THE MANY ISLANDS

THE MANY ISLANDS

POEMS BY

WILLIAM GOODREAU

Atheneum New York 1961

Acknowledgment is made to the following periodicals for permission to reprint poems originally appearing in them: *Chicago Choice, Colorado Quarterly, The Commonweal, The Critic, Hudson Review.*

Library of Congress catalog card number 61-9255
Published simultaneously in Canada by Longmans, Green & Company
Manufactured in the United States of America by H. Wolff, New York
Designed by Harry Ford
First Edition

CONTENTS

MISTER HAYDN   *2*

COUNTRY CHILDREN   *3*

A VERSE LETTER   *4*

SOME FACETS OF LOVE   *5*

THREE POEMS FOR THREE NUNS   *6*

LEGENDS OF GRIEF   *9*

A SONG   *13*

THE STORM   *14*

THE QUESTION PUT TO THE ARTIST
    AND THE ANSWER SHE GAVE   *15*

MOZART TAKES A STROLL   *17*

SO GROWS THE TREE   *18*

SNOW   *19*

BETTY THE SKATER   *20*

YOUR FORTUNE   *22*

THE LAMP   *23*

OBJECT LESSON   *24*

HIS FIRST CONFESSION   *25*

THE ADULTERER'S PROMISE   *26*

AT HER GRAVE   *27*

THE QUIZ *28*

TO HIS MISTRESS *29*

CHANGE IS MY THEME *30*

THE FATHER *31*

Francis Jammes: THE POOR SOLDIER *32*

A HORROR STORY *33*

VALENTINE *34*

THE YOUNG FISHERMAN'S FUNERAL
ON MONHEGAN *35*

PAINT *38*

A SEA MEDITATION *39*

Francis Jammes: WHEN WILL I SEE
THE ISLANDS *41*

TELEMACHOS *42*

RIVER POEM *43*

FIRST BUCOLIC *44*

JUBILATE *46*

THE QUEST *48*

CONCERNING THE SOUL *49*

DAVID IS MARK ANTONY . . . *50*

FATHER SEBASTIEN RALE, S.J.—
A LETTER TO HIS BROTHER *53*

The Lord is King: let the earth exult,
let the many islands be glad.

PSALM *96*

THE MANY ISLANDS

It is not December; Mr. Haydn sighs.
Outside the maple trees have crowns of honey,
And children, looking up into the leaves,
See crowds of sunny fish float on the sky.
But Haydn wishes he might see fresh snow
Falling in the gardens, gliding down
The shoulders of a Daphne or a tree.
He blows upon his fingers until his mind
Is cold. Amber clusters touch his eyes.
His abstract score is hurled into the light,
Its rhythms swarmed with clots of wine and gold.
Why should dark cellos storm into his vision
Like swarms of bees about a honeycomb?

When we were children taking buggy rides
By farms stinging with odors of dark earth,
We looked at windmills hardly going round,
At clouds which seemed immobile as soft hills.
If we were girls we thought about bright beads
We'd caught a glimpse of in the jewelry store.
If we were boys we talked about the horse,
Could write its name. West Union, Iowa
Was not to blame. Our cousin's satin skirt,
The coins in Grandpa's leather purse inflamed
Our shining brows. It was as if a rain
Had filled the open hillocks of the brain
And seeded slender herbs and shapely trees.

Today, the slow corruption of those dreams
Snows lightly on our frame house and its yard.
It drifts about our mother's scent, her furs;
And drives against our father's polished hearse.

My dearest friend, I cannot take my leave
Of attitudes which tend to make a fog
Of all I've ever dreamed. I touch no sleeve
That folds upon an angel's arm. I flog

Imagination in the darkest cell
Of my deserted brain. I hear no owl
In terrifying rage and fear no spell.
The angel now encumbered by his cowl

Looks out upon a black unmoving sea.
Back home in Maine the garden's nearly lost:
The roses buried in dry maple leaves,
The zinnias and asters chewed with frost.

And even here, the Mississippi spills
Its muddy surface in my narrow veins
Until my blood in numbness hurls my will
Against a mind so stubborn speech is killed.

I seem to be a cave where sullen wolves
Refuse to breed or hide from hunters' dogs.
There is no point to pray to be absolved,
Since I am digging out my rooted God.

Lately in the garden and in the starlight
We have been singing over and over again
Our delight in love. Tangled in images looped
Through warm living-room windows—yellow lamps,
Shadows of lilac upon the shutters, the mist,
The coming together of brooks with flooded banks—
We embrace. We fall back in the shining wet woods,
And float through delicate webs and budding limbs,
While stars, crystals of snow and wires of rain
Sing in our blood. We float over inlets, bogs
And tidal streams to the fluttering sea whose wings
Beat over us until we have the taste of flesh
And blood, the hunger for golden visions.

THREE POEMS FOR THREE NUNS

I

You will ride a donkey gray as any dove,
And some fool in moth-chewed motley
With eyes too brown and feet too large
Will ring down towers in Petworth town
For your coming. The dusty road will roll
Clouds of smoke before you. A wise buffoon—
A heap of bone—with needle and thread
Of Magdalen's hair will stitch bells of mink
About your mantle and your thin serge veil.

Nones will be a little out of tune,
And the Father will imitate your laughter.

Tu, ma soeur, will be held by a real hand—
Salut Marie—
                    having been raised from a platinum cage
To float without wings,
                    but surrounded by numberless wings
That shall be ultra-marine,
                    speckled by topaz and jet
And scented with roses
                    that have been waiting long
On the milk-blue feet
                    of the blinding diamond peacock.

Nones will be a Bach Partita;
The Father will have you rock the Child.

I have met nymphs and satyrs
Always adorable, even the steeds of Aeneas
When they were ponies; but not until now
Have I met the nun who wears a wimple
Cut of the unicorn's flesh, a scapular
Made of the doe's.
                  You are dangerous
Because you know Saint Francis' agony
And tenderness with grinning wolves,
Because you feed his blooded body without clothes.

No angel will be late for Nones.
The Father shall weep, astonished by your eyes.

1. *The Son*

He begged for bruises of decay,
A fever and green stakes of pain,
Since grace would come no other way.

His words spill out
Like loose change
From a worn-out pocket.
In a living-room or restaurant
Dreams slip over him like waves
That lap a sandy stretch of shore.
All that he thought is worn
Into that sand. And terror
Trickles down the bare slopes of his brain.

2. *Threnody*

*Secrets, then, have to be taken
Into the bouquets you made.*

*The flowers grew well by the sea
And flourished in the salt wind's blowing.*

*Even so, some petals were always broken
Before the blossoms were brought together,
Arranged, . . . before the day was over.*

3. *The Father*

The snow is crusted, pitted
With ashes. Smoke from chimneys
Is crookedly twisting through the sky.
The house, slanting toward a maze
Of iron trees, hears bells sounding
From the hidden winter sea.
                                    My father
Walks through dark rooms of his house,
Unwilling to light a lamp or draw
A shade. He will not look at purple
Colors in the rug or touch
The heavy mirror's walnut frame.

He stabs the wooden cupboard doors
Crying, "I will never die."
We force him to his single bed
And face a solid, papered wall.

4. *The Daughter*

She prays God not to throw her away,
Begs Him light the rounded curve
Of the sea's horizon with a tiny sun,
That she might burn off these ashes
And rest someplace God's image lingers.

She cannot dream of death, but of sparkling
Seeds that sprout in the soil's deep night,
The fresh plumage of trees, the frail birch
Curving like a silver rib of light.

5. *The Mother*

Sudden as her sickness there appeared
Bodies of flame in frenzy near her grave.
Rising as high as trees, their burning seared
Yards of rolling haze. Thin voices raved

And crackled in the sod and rooted nerve.
She heard them grind her wishes for the dead
Naked in the sockets of their flame; then swerve
Upon her mind until it choked and bled.

6. Envoi

Bring out the things
Your grief has stored away
In so many hated boxes.
What was that bowl to you,
That the silver of its rounded shell
Should be packed away
And never filled with water?—
Never to reflect the edge
And curl of leaves, unfurling
Beards of purple iris,
Or the fine gold of summer light?

When you were younger, birds came down
And ate from your hand. You stood with me,
Your skirt wound in the wind. A frown—
Love's spoiled sense of melody—
Embraced the sugar-maple trees
And flashed like sun on paper leaves.

You touched my other world not trying,
And forced my eyes to peck the ground
Just like a bird. I saw the crying
And the pout of all my years surround
The fluent grass and form a gird.
Your smile had fed a host of birds.

Your body moves with clocking sun,
Extravagant in yellow light.
And my wild fingers pale to run
Against your deep brown hair. The bright
Memory of that day stands still.
You were younger, locked to my will.

THE STORM

Because a freezing rain had slashed the town,
It bleeds with stiff and polished ice. The sea
Is thrown against the wind. The lines are down.
There is no light. By morning I should hear
Whose fishing boat was smashed, what neighbor drowned.

But sorrow is needed. Greek choruses tell us that.
Reading their singing strophes in my flat
Beside a lamp that reeks of kerosene,
I watch the tragic pattern death combats
Smoulder in the green part of the flame.
It throws my shadow in a kind of dance
Across the floor in rhythms all the same
As drowned men's cries, with wind's, with sea's advance.

THE QUESTION PUT TO THE ARTIST
AND THE ANSWER SHE GAVE

What is it?
What is it you think about?

"I don't know what it is. I know
It's in everything I think about: in peppers cut
So they display a variorum text on green,
In linens that are white, so clean that they annul
Their whiteness in a kind of sheen
Of reds and blues; it's in chimney smoke
That blows dove-gray and holds an aspect
Of the sun, in oranges that shine and glass that seres
The taste of coffee and the oil of cream."

"I cannot say I *think* of any one of these
But that they are and so are just as real
As what inhabits me.
                              I watch the sea
Which is more than wholly of this globe—
The shape, the place reflecting in its stars,
The face of the moon, its vacant smile."

"It's not of War I think about, but of blood
Dried on stone, of voices that have no origins
In themselves, of pinks that scent
Quick ladies' poems written for Troy and Rome
In those towns which glow in the thighs
Of old mountains in northern Italy
And Ecuador.

I remember a cat
That keeps her home in the Forum and a cat
That sleeps in an empty June cafe,
And a cat starving in Egypt
And drowned in a bag dropped into the bay.
And the child born in the theatre;
The look of a corpse—its expectation and its loss."

"It's in the soil I sift through my hand
Imagining Adonis and the boar.
It is in the swirl of the void
That calls thunder over the house in August
And pulls me from my bed to sketch the sky's
Canopy shifting, even rent with the storms
That shall never occur again in the same way
Except in my mind.
      It is the cruelty inflicted
On the entirely beautiful and their refusal
Not to stop believing in the graces of the sun:
The eye, the lion, the dolphin, that holds our image—
Whether blooming, fading or dead—alive."

"My dear—
I would not be looking if I knew what it is—
Neither would I love the casement of this window
That frames you as you cry; nor would I think
To carve this furrow in the Sibyl's ivory brow."

Mozart walks under sets of trees
Perfecting symphonies which glow
Like Cherubino's airy mind—
Unembarrassed at the flow
Of languorous emotion.

He has forgotten winters of romance,
Betrayals and chance glimpses
Of lovers cruelly exposed;

For much of that would seem to rest
In carriages which sped to chilling halls
With tapestries thrown over broken thrones,
In letters he had written upside down,
In the pity of his wearing courtly clothes.

Flowering in this atmosphere of trees,
Mozart breaks the solitude of clouds,
The shaded images of moonless hell,
And sings with no regard for love that sweeps
The majesty of mind into a heap
Of worlds against a woman's breast or mouth.

Let Cherubino pine in icy lace and hose!

A shining limb, the sky, blossoms and stars
Flow away. This music trembles all alone.
Its fluid measure lifts through galaxies and spheres,
Touching quiet minds with lustrous tears.

Just for a time the green filigree
Of Time in the sun's hand will lose its grip
And tip the pointed ladder in the tree.
Your father's pocket-watch will stop and slip

Behind the clouds. And you will say, "His tick-
And-tock has ended. Let us duly pray."
At that time you'll leave your work to nick
The heart carved in the tree, giving away

Your place about the foliage and heat
Of early day. The sun will fall through leaves
Like lead fruit tumbling at your weathered feet,
Crashing in pastureland. Then Time will cleave

Above your father's grave. Left far behind
In rows of hollyhock and vine you'll wake
Your dreaming bride while sun and moon unwind.
You'll teach your boy to climb the tree and break

Through limbs of Time. And it will strike you then,
As clocks the hour, how children shake you free
And shock the sun. How all broad daylight bends
In one enormous arc to grip this tree.

Wide snow falls gently,
Dulling the picket fence,
Rounding the rough granite wall.

Snow is as gentle as moonlight
Falling in a blue night; careful
As the embrace of lovers
Who are fast asleep, dreaming one dream:
For snow reshapes everything,
Even the fibrous stocks
Of winter-bitten hollyhocks.
The snow releases hills,
Letting them slide to muddy roads,
To matted pastures, swamps and ponds.

I have seen stark, uncanny shapes
Twisted from rocks, cottage roofs and roots—
All of delicate snow. And I have been loved
Wading in the vast dreams of snow.

BETTY THE SKATER

I

Betty the skater, ankles bent, would stop
And sink in snow. Her icy hands would free
The strings which laced her, would press back the blood
That bumped along her veins. With nets of trees
She'd scrape the gloved and buckled hearts that preened
The white-splashed ice. And those that moved in circles
Would wield a wind which melted her gray eyes—
She would be the glove a swift-skater held, a bell
Which jumped on girded hair. She would be the lover.

II

"It is cold in the night sky. The tree
Has bled. O God, the tree has bled.
My watery blood has made a pond
Where lovers skate. Beneath
This tree, these limbs, I hang my love
Naked for birds of spring to take.
I die to melt and run free again
Like the surge that breathes the melted ice."

Betty the skater weeps in bed
And spins the globe on Atlas. Forced
To dream, she chases gold-cuffed birds
That float in a reed pool. Their wings
Are mottled-blue and spread like floats
That Cleopatra rides. She throws
Her unfurled arms out straight and spins
To press them near. In their eyes real black
Is set. They slap the water, whack
Up waves that lave her thighs. She breaks
Those fettered wings, and drinks the blood.

I see you in a dark cellar,
Sitting at a round table,
Drinking concoctions
You have never seen before.
You are being introduced
To venerable men
Who are very much at home.
They have white beards,
And speak of relatives
And rainy winters spent
With no work in the shops.
They tell of looking at
The Merrimac, at broken
Slabs of floating ice,
Of not wanting to climb
The icy sidewalk home.
They could tell of driving
To Crawford Notch, of raising
Flocks of chickens, of building
Summer cottages;
But, for you, the better thing
To know is how it was
When, at seventeen,
Your mother was coughing blood.

Lighting the lamp and setting it
Before the glass reduced the world
To the edges of this room; the stars
Were washed away, even the trees
That brushed the house were absent now.
Except for the splash of the rising sea,
The tired sounding of a bell,
Our entry here became the sum
Of every certainty. The windows
Mirrored solid walls and frames
Of gold that held still violent seas,
Fish-houses and gray, leaning docks,
But closed us off from what was real
Until we broke into ourselves
And opened lonesome wounds that shone
On solid landscapes, wild and green.

Actually the truth of anything
Is purposeless, unless it has a setting,
Has a house which was built
Beside huge trees and gardens
With vegetables and many flowers—that is,
A place where things can happen.
No room can be empty or very clean.
There should be chairs that need
Reupholstery, having faded in the sun,
And objects brought home at some expense
From a silversmith in Amsterdam,
From the estate of an aunt
You never cared about—a mahogany
Chest or secretary that was stained.

Rooms should be arranged to accommodate
The angry, the ugly and the dull.
They should be places where,
If you are in love, you may enter
And touch the fabric of a drape
Or the glaze of something porcelain
And be contained.

I

With dust hemming their full black skirts
Nuns sit us in the empty church.
They whisper through the tick of beads
While gothic shadows dim our heads.
Afraid to look wide-eyed for sin
I count the altar-steps and squint
Through stained-glass saints in royal-blue.
I bite the varnish from the pew.

The confession-box gives off no light
But just a rough outline of Christ.

II

O Sisters, do you know how grim
He is alone with sin? And how
He dare not turn should he forget
Confession's speech? He breathes the wood
Of cedar, pressed against the screen
As if the dark could capture him
And blind his eyes for good.
                                            Father,
You start to see a child this still
Look up so wildly asking penance.
Your absolution's like some flame
That beats back on itself in shame.

One day, the high waves vanished,
The salt taste gone from our mouths . . .
The serpent weed and frosted crests
Of breakers gone as well, I shall walk
Through you as bell sounds tear
Through granite walls, shattering the posture
Which this strict devotion to your married life
Freezes into you. And the north wind,
Carrying snow from other islands, will cover us.
The clean scent of berries and fir
Will drive into our wasted blood
While whale-dark clouds weight down and quiet
The wild condition of our love.

For Edna St. Vincent Millay

Suffering for your doom, I come unknown
To you, possessing nothing as hard as stone
Or rugged as the shoreline is. Your blood
And grave shall keep us unattached through years
Of mud and rain. We are joined as the island you owned
Is joined to winter seas . . . by nothing more.

Atlantic winds, tearing down steepled trees,
Made you lascivious, quite sick with your dreams.
Then the first ragged dandelion cut deeply in you
As it did in winter's cold light and sparse snow.
Now your face, poisoned by the naked sore of grief,
Cries out in unremitting loneliness.

In Austerlitz' icy name you built the retreat
That could not bury Camden's living warmth—
The address on Washington Street, the nasturtium's flame,
Blue hills lifting you through that seaport's haze.
It cannot hurt your name to think you failed;
I have watched the hacking of seas on broken sails.

Suppose an angel slipped down on a rope
Of twisting silk and landed in a tree
In front of your white porch, a telescope
Fixed to his side and maps spread on his knee.

Now would you trample down the wooded stairs
And stand within the shadow of his wings?—
Demand he quite your property and scare
Yourself with a furied mind's imagining?

Perhaps you'll take those treasured maps outright
Believing other hemispheres are there
Encompassed on that chart. Or will you crowd

The glass against your eye and fiercely stare
Across the mountain ridge and through white cloud
Into a lion's roar of perfect light?

I like you best unclothed
As if loosed from clinging sin,
Where sunlight makes you gold
And shadows fill white folds
On this squawking featherbed,
Where love does not wear thin.
Like salmon schools enthralled
By forest lakes ahead

You brace the heart and scale
Hidden currents of my soul.
I race wide-eyed to shed
What lovers fiercely dread—
Manner's belt and robes
Of speech, conceits' plaid stole,
And dreams concealed in veils—
To dress a naked globe.

A noisy bed too old,
A yawning money-cat
Outside the bedroom door,
Vest our surface shore.
You wish for torrent light,
And push a streaming slat.
We brazenly behold
Love, innocent of night.

You will be taken now
Into the bough of spring which is an arm
You used to know and dwell upon.
And whatever flowers are there—white with a wax of pink
Or wet with something close to blue—
Accept without comparison. Forget
What the Japanese might do with them,
What Renoir would turn them to.

Lean down and watch the brook swimming on
The shadow of this walnut tree. Allow
The sun to slide from leaves upon your wrists,
To shiver in a silver tangle on this stream.

Whose hair or limbs this world might be
Has little consequence. What stones mark
Is birth or death. The branching roots that vein
This soil and drink in the flash of sudden rain
Are myth enough. See how against this sky the bark
Draws toward itself the strongest blue, knits
To its darkest edge the mystery of what we view.

The scent of snowdrops clustering, the swift
Assault of clouds, stir your deepest calm;
But what is more than this comes not from you.
It burns through vacant sockets of the dead,
And feeds the mind its coarsest, blackest bread.

This only child adjusts the dream you fathered
At your leisure in this clean suburban town.
The room you added, all that decor gathered
For the world of little boys. A kind of crown

Put on your house to show its growing up.
You look upon the public lake, its shore
And pathway neat as brushwork on a cup.
Calm on the screened-in porch you dwell before

That comforting green and breathe a sigh as still
As water on the lake. So much, you say . . .
So much. Your house is white, the windows filled
With antique amber glass. And Saturday

The time's your son's. Night coolness stirs
Great elms which shade the park, a shadow strays
Beyond the lake, across the hills and blurs
Into the blank gold moon. Your hair is gray.

After Francis Jammes

The poor soldier meekly said: My eyes
Are very poor, my right arm's paralysed.

Poor devil—he has no mother, certainly.
She'd bring some comfort in this misery.

He lives like that, a soldier in a tin,
His moist hand wiping his brow, now and then.

On the bank he makes a pillow of his arms.
Falling asleep he's a little child and calm.

His tunic lacks a pillow's cleanliness,
It fades against his full beard's dirty crest.

He must be frugal just to live a day.
He's so distressed. What would he give to bathe?

He wraps himself in threadbare cloth which drapes
Completely round the wretched body of an ape.

The poor soldier meekly said: My eyes
Are very poor, my right arm's paralysed.

I saw the curtains fold in billows,
Breaking the stems of violets on the sill.

I saw fires break out in every room:
The mad rage of the father, his fist
Ripped on the broken mirror, his teeth
Grinding on the black manna of despair.
I watched his youngest daughter
Bringing fire from the cold cellar.
I heard the slow gasping for air
Of the mother who could no longer swallow water.

Who buttoned up the children's winter coats?
Who pinched color into their belly-white faces?

A spinster aunt came down from Lawrence
And breathed into their faces. Her skirts
Had a musty smell. Her teeth were not her own.

This valentine needs all outdoors
Not rooms with brightly furnished floors.
For I have done away with lace,
Smooth gilded hearts and Cupid's face.
I've found distaste in painted birds,
Forget-me-nots and cut-out words.
For all of this my love is less
And does not merit soul's address.
I'd rather see you walking slow
Through banking paths of winter snow,
Alone upon a field so white
That stars would pull toward the light—
Or standing near a tree entwined
With delicately tapered vines
Consider how our two soul's graft
Upon love's world-supporting staff
And drift above cold snow and ice
Into a scarlet paradise.

So I send nothing but my voice,
Bare as the winter hills, by choice.

THE YOUNG FISHERMAN'S FUNERAL
ON MONHEGAN

1. *The Body*

The dark blue of the salt-box room
Spread out until it seemed to touch
The undulations in the cove and hide
The littered beach—the stones and broken shells,
Discarded lobster traps and weed.
For here the corpse reclines as it never had
In life, tight in its dark-blue suit,
French cuffs and tie.
                    Living, was he ignorant
Of this rite that plants eyes, colored
As the sea, deep in dry Monhegan soil?

2. *His Wife*

She observes the Atlantic ocean
From Burnt Head—a lofty rock
Shaped like a monk's black hood
Hardened by dark glacial storms.
Looking down its forehead
She tastes the mist which hangs
Like silk above the knifing surf.
She watches the sea swinging mountains of weight,
Hurling them at this grave enormous cliff.
The thunder-clap of wave on wave
Hacks her memory to ruin.
Old dreams collapse, swallowed
By these purple jaws. Chairs and tables,
A crib and painted lamps spin under waves.
And she, upon this boldest stone,
Drifts with that wreckage,
Beyond the whitest village, totally alone.

3. *Her Prayer*

Well, you were drunk
And bled out of your ears.
Your truck hadn't started that morning,
So you cursed my name
And ran behind the store to find your brother.

I wouldn't have let you touch me
All that night if you had lived.
I hated your eyes flooded with fire.
Even the tourists came to your funeral.
Jane's voice filled your coffin
With all the love your family deserved.

4. *The Other Man: A Painter*

We surrendered to the fog
Left with the room and fire,
The moan of horns and cry of gulls.
All distance was erased, but we were more aware
Of what we could not see—the saw-edge line
Of fir that tears across the sky,
The wet stone, the yellow masts.

Damp in that vacancy of mist
And dark, I molded the setting
In which we kissed.

PAINT

You might think up questions to be asked
Of colors—how they last:
How yellows, grays rub off like chalk and change
With even bites of wet
And salt. How white paint breaks, is crazed and runs
Toward an unbleached haze
Of sun. You see this when your house-front banks
Against a near-white cloud
Or hangs its shadow through light swabs of snow.
Most colors die inside the year.
We've only gardens which amass hard color
To the pitch and blast of
Sea weather. It is for these perennials
We scrape our neutral door.

On this day when sunlight lichens us
With amber drops, we tend to dream for the sea
Who, without imagination, inhales and sleeps
Upon powers that issue extraordinary facts—
The luminous flanks of mackerel and cod,
Languorous trees with gentle beckoning hands
Of green and iodine, and blues so various . . .
So true that we compose litanies of their names.

Is it glory for man to let the sea play chords
And runs on this most delicate instrument: the mind?
Flattering ourselves, we think this consciousness
Seraphic in its roll. But instrument it is, indeed . . .
Dependent, secret, and when alone, most afeared.

You who swim Hooker's green waves, although close
To shore, you have sensed the danger, disrespect
And law imposed by surf, by sudden whorls
And dragon undertow. From soul's dark floor,
Panic, like the octopus, puffs up inky clouds;
Its tentacles and suckers draw your courage dry.
You cough the sea that coughs you to the shore.

At such moments—others come in swallowing fogs,
In vessels beyond the lightship's horn and cone,
In isolated coves—the rain is pitiless.

Swells spill vomit from your acid throat.
The world thunders out of time,
Bursting gunwales and keel,
Exposing brutishly
That self you do not pack and store in chests
Of healthy skull and bone. *Here* you know the sea.

The mind hollowed like Atlantic shells,
Repeats, translates, records these sheathes of surf,
Unknotted by who knows what gods; then, drowns,
Dissolving on airy shocks and spores of brine.

But still we dream our passions in this sea.
Floating on eerie depths beyond cold bells,
Lonely as the distant crying of the gull,
We beg the sea to buoy our human dreams,
To tug their shapes, to wash them in her swells.

After Francis Jammes

When will I see the islands where my parents were?
Before the port, the ocean, under stars
Men smoked cigars and dressed in faded blue,
A negro strummed guitar and in the court
Rainwater fell asleep in quiet pools.
The sea was like a bouquet wound with tule
And night-time sad as summer and a flute.
Men smoked their black cigars with the red tips
Glowing round them, looking like nesting birds
Which certain gifted poets tell about.
O Father of us all, you were there, before
My soul was even born, guiding these sloops
To leeward through the vast colonial night.
Now as you thought of lighting your cigar,
And while a negro played a sad guitar,
Did my soul, which wasn't born, exist at all?
Could it have been guitar or the sloop's white sail?
Was it the motion of a bird's little head
Hidden on the grounds of some plantation?
Or a black fly's heavy flight inside a mansion?

TELEMACHOS

Caught again in this damp sameness
He desires nothing. He hears the gull
Answer the buoy, not seeing either topple
In low waves. Sensing only
The immensity of his own burden
Expansive as the fog—the impossible
That is accepted, the dampness that weighs down
The wind, woods that draw back
With no branch locking, leaf falling—
He exerts the language and the tongue
Becoming to Athena who should bring
A boy to wisdom on a blazing shore.

Sorrow beyond sorrow is yours, passed by
In the river's mirroring face. That lady stooping,
Gathering violets, makes a picture
With the green river shadowed on both sides.
So does her beau in the white flannel pants.
Their courtship resumes. But theirs are sorrowful eyes,
For there is Time to consider, moveable Time.
Further down there are violets near an oak
Cut down some twenty years or so. One might
Stop there . . . where a belltower like Wren's
Looks picturesque. Where the story they tell is myth.
How a girl was waiting prim in organdy
When picnickers, children and all, came by
And made her cry. She hid by the mulberry tree
And was involved in double suicide.
But no. You can't mark sorrow just by place,
Or where children in red-piped Sunday coats
Hang to their mother's hand and walk these banks.
It's a thing beyond this. Reflected. Like trees
Bending green boughs full with yellow sun,
Weaving an arbor or darkness and shadow across
The length of this course. A double water-image.
A young man fixed between reflective eyes.

I

On seeing Theocritus in Sicily
Wound in praise of Amaryllis, his emotion
Curled around the memory of white
Limbs, even bone, that are wax,—we are moved.

II

Priapus leaps from vein to vein.
                              Nijinsky
Pastes his face, is tearing his mask.
The body is formed, is hurled into reality
Made from thousands of watts and the faun's beige.
So. The teeth do sweat.
                        We claim much;
And watch, unmoved, the boy grow senile
In his youth.
                No poplars rot beside his grave.
No cypress twists its strength of limb, bends
With thunder cloud, electric shock or younger trees.

III

My lord, who struggled in Apollo,
Blossomed on a heap of straw,
Warmed by dung; was fed by a virgin
Girl who knew nothing of pearls
And mourning tides: she feared her child.

44

IV

Praise Arcady
And the granite
Which holds the victim to his phrase.

Play flutes, resplendent in their springs
Of tone, running under cliffs
And painted wheels, upon the altar
For which a star was ground to meal.

Sing the Daphnis whose respect
Unfolds and tangles waves and waves
Of loosened hair, Chloe's smile.

V

It is only power, the amazing,
Which cants to the sky—the voice
Deepened by the comfort of clouds,
The sun slanted to the shepherd's face
Is rose—taking us back and forth
From light to dark, from mind to heart,
Fixing us to the least of creeds.

Part of a feather blows
Against a bank of flowers,
Is caught against a stem.

My mind embraces both—
Feather and flower—
And does not think to choose.
It is local, and aroused
To praise a stretch of trees,
Rising on granite layers,
Backed against the sea.

I do not ask how can this fit?
Nor do I say, this has nothing
To do with feathers and flowers
In a garden that is one mile
East of the place where I've watched
The ocean strike the shore.
I know the temper of the sea
Which has much to do with the cry
Of gulls as well as with the shaping
Of trees, the building of cliff.
I've watched granite lock its head
With the roll and drive of the surf;
And seen the gull in flight
As it approaches groves of evergreen,

While the cerulean tide
Climbs the rock toward trees,
Merging like a garden
Across the forest floor,
Spouting bushy trees, all white,
Upon the grave emblazoned sky.

Our God made nothing that is common.
Yet there is no feather, spruce or petal
That can live without some sharp vein
Of some thing more than what it is.

And I am wet with all that spray.

If after all, roses deceive us
Because of their attachment to an overrated
Myth—the vision of the bower
Made permanent in plotted excursions
Through elevated regions where there are
Numerous groves, calm streams, and many examples
Of fine architecture upon wide plains
Of mossy green—we should not
Avoid the possible value that their inspection
Would render the betrayed mind.

(Considering the lion or leviathan,
The hunt or the raising of good Lazarus
Spread before us on a tapestry
Of meaningless devices, we are forced to wonder
In public, and that is probably enough.)

But if the rose, by reason, bears
No import on the vast dissension of our time,
Regardless how it climb and cluster in the yard
Or unfold one morning we would disregard,
Who will explain it subject for the dream
Where we depart less substance than a cloud
For an ordinary place in which we can't believe
Where there are roses carefully arranged
The way we'd thought they always should have been?

The soul is able to take
Long walks by the oceanside,
Walks that involve crawling
Over cold rock while open
To the danger of tides
And slippery mops of weed.

One's soul should not be shocked by lights
That wheel upon it in the dark and glare
Upon its awkwardness; nor should foghorns
Turn it away, make it swear or close its eyes.

No soul must be awful.
It cannot ignore the green
Sea throwing patches of foam
Against hulls of ships that are
Clearly geometrical. It must
Ring with the buoys, let itself
Be slapped with waves and salt.
And it should look at islands
For what they are—places where
People can't live, summer ended.

Mark Antony, showy in his leather gear,
Swept monumental through your liquid halls—
Inside your chamber kicked his sandals off
And swore he was death-sick of fighting wars.

In that rich ambiguous bed, he theorized
His happy death. While petulance, to taste
The peel, the pulp and core of love, outshone
The icy glittering of double stars.

And when he died his armour was so prized.
It fell so luminous, white from his arms.
As queen you gathered in Death's horrid robes,
Pressing your mouth upon its dusty hem.

Still, David glanced upon your roof one time
And could not leave. Your flesh tore through his flesh
Like some bedazzled fish, splashing his mind.
One giant wish to weight you with a crown

Put out the rhythmic music in his eyes
Before he threw himself to bramble flames.
His fasting filled your womb with desert fruit;
It bent the boughs of Jesse's silver tree.

But David is Mark Antony. On this
I'll swear. For men will always quit a war
To fight on greater scale. These men explode
The apple on the tree and show its scar.

They kiss a different girl and sleep before
Their time. Some say lauds and others beads.
But all stand under that same tree and try
One magnificent gesture before they die.

FATHER SEBASTIEN RALE, S.J.
A LETTER TO HIS BROTHER

Injuriam facit Martyri qui orat pro eo . . . —St. Augustine

Father Sebastien Rale was a French Jesuit sent to New
France in 1689 as a missionary. He labored among the Indians of Illinois and Maine. He was murdered by the British
in 1724 at Narantsouak (Norridgewalk, Maine).

A Narantsouak, ce Octobre 1723.

Monsieur et Très-Cher Frère,
        La paix de N. S.

During these thirty years of ardor spent
Au milieu forêts avec les Sauvages,
I have been so occupied instructing them
In Christian virtue, dogma and in prayer
That I have had scarce leisure to write,
Even to you who are most dear to me.
Still, I cannot refuse the little account
You ask—that, *in fact, I owe*
In gratitude for the Love your letters show.

The village in which I dwell is called
Narantsouak: stoutly built
On the bank of a river, which runs
Into the sea not far below.
Besides a commodious Church, so well adorned
To be esteemed in France, two Chapels stand
On paths leading to fields and the shaded wood.
The Savage never fails to pause
A moment before these shrines. . . .

Sometimes

I pray my work will save these souls
And my own soul. I've learned to take
Their salty fish, ground acorn meal,
The pumpkin mash and sickly corn.
I've gone like a mascot on the Bay
And built an altar over rocks
While Indians died to head me off
From British troopers' scarlet red . . .
And Yankee traders giving a rien
For winter's pile of heavy fur.
Like trees they fall . . . but do not fall.
I see myself crush down their earth.

I have trained a minor clergy
Of forty young males,
Who, in cassock and surplice, assist
At Divine Service. Each has his duty
Not only serving me at Mass,
But chanting the Divine Office
Before the Blessed Sacrament, and in Processions—
Which are made with a great concourse of Savages.

If I could only bring them Christ
And not myself, ainsi:
In August when they said New France
Was not bound by the Kennebec
I trembled with a chipmunk's rage
And had my children throw them back . . .
My Chief, his wife, depend for word,
For breath. They will not hunt or fish

Unless I try their traps and nets.
I had them burn revenge across
Those pilgrim fields—pillage by fire
Each house and barn.

We're forty leagues
From British coastal settlements.
This proximity, at first, somewhat pleased
The Savage not seeing the bald trap
Set for him and thinking only of the stores
Where he might trade. But at last
Seeing how fast the English villages
Surrounded him, he asked them by what right
They settled on his land and even built
Forts therein, and some of stone . . .
La réponse qu' on lui fit savoir,
Que le Roi de France avait cédé
Son pays au Roi d'Angleterre,
Le jeta dans de plus grandes alarmes.
They came at once to me.

I said
Their hamlet's given for you to eat.
And now a price upon my scalp!—
They say one-thousand pounds and still
Contend "the jesuit"
Upsets the Treaty of Utrecht
So they can mark King George fine trees
And push the "aborigines"
Off the islands' fertile shores,
From river bank and salmon falls,

Then jam their whale-boats deep inland—
Build a block-house . . . take command
Of the great forests the river feeds
With one iron cannon ball.

Far dearer than the trade
The British could provide
Is the Faith the Savage holds,
And they believe to break with me
Would leave them without
Priest and Sacrifice.
My attempt to confirm the Savage
In his Faith is the King's great obstacle.

Each day I find myself alone
Along the river's edge, back far
Enough so not to see myself
Grow in among the sumac leaves
And stripling cedars rushing on
The river's face. I think I see
Another face: my youngest Brave's,
Who will go off in that first snow,
Northward where my forest bell
Will never ring. He'll climb the rock
And ankle-wearing cliffs which rise
Into Katahdin's winter jaw
Of never-thawing ice and prove
His youth and worthiness.

But I should tell you of the land.
Each year on Assumption Day

We harvest beans, corn and squash
Which lasts until all Hallows Eve.
At this time we leave for the Sea.
Besides large fish, shell fish and fruit
We find bustard, duck and all sorts of game—
They cover the water like the green islands
On which we camp, where I bless the bounty.
By Purification Day all but the Hunters return.
They stalk the foraging bear, elk and deer.

But I no longer love the world
As I had thought. I sense its change
In me for what I brought
To rack against this sky
Where arrows strike their mark.
                               My hands
Pull Christ from his own bark and lathe
Away the proper bend and knot,
Lop off gray boughs and twist new leaves
Easily as a white canoe
Slides on flushing water.

Oh Satan, I am clawed by you!

I've given up the hope of France:
Nor do I care whose cannon drums
Into the red wound of the sun,
Whose timber falls against the axe,
Whose foxes bark in iron traps.
A thousand sacred breads have fouled
All but the stench and salve of fire.

Some years ago the most able man among
The ministers of Boston came
At the foot of our river that he might teach
The children of the Savage. Neglecting nothing
He sought the children out and flattered them.
He made them little presents and put to them
Questions concerning their Faith, and then,
From answers made to him, he turned
Into derision, the Sacraments,
Purgatory, the invocation of the Saints,
The beads, crosses, lights and
Images we piously observe.

I dream they'll fill their hate
Into my eyes and throat with fists
Of pitch and mud; then prop me dead
Against a Church of broken bone
Which falls apart in lonely flame.

I dream my throat is white and bleeds.

I sent direct a Memoir to his school.
Some fifty pages proved
By Scripture and Tradition
Those Articles he dare attack by jest.

A wild laurel . . .

What's in a man
To sprinkle holy water when
You've preached your warriors to death?

It was that day I came across the hill
When Colonel Westbrook with his men
Had torn out from the river bank,
Then stormed with flame and bolting guns
Upon my Chapel, screaming, "Blood
Of Romish Rale, of Popery!"
Some angel gave me time to cross,
Attending me until I knew
I'd only given death to show
His consecrated bread and hold
This wood-burnt soul.
                    I hid in time
And swallowed every wafered host
Which I had blessed for week-day Mass.

A girl screamed for her black-robed priest;
A silent tongue gagged her throat.
A boy panicked in the fields;
His father's blood spat on his skin.
While black pellets battered Death
The glutton of the sacred bread
Ate with lust, with Adam's greed
That final yeast—viaticum.

I heard a *Dies Irae* spin
Like gnats around unbandaged wounds . . .
And fainting, heard my father's voice
The day I left the Norman shores . . .
Those billowing sails, the keen winds
Biting my eyes. . . .
                    My cassock singed

And steamed. I swallowed every host
For every soul that had God's need.
I choked Christ's blessed body dead
Until my hollow throat seemed red.
I saw the bayberry candles melt
Across the altar cloth and smelled
My body's stench . . . I scrambled free
Sprawling beneath the evergreens.

I walked upon that ravagement
Absolvant des enfants morts.

A wild laurel borders the islands
Bearing fruit in Fall like the juniper tree.
They hang in such great clusters
One Savage can gather four minots a day,
From which I obtain ten livres of wax
And supply the Church with innumerable lights.

I shook the Chapel bell in tears
And cried Revenge! into their ears;
Then blessed each Brave that left that night. . . .

They took my books, my breviary,
My little tin of China tea.
The dictionary by which I thought
My Indian parish would be taught
The mysteries of church and cross.

In Spring the maple-tree contains a fluid
Which trickles down the trunk to vessels of bark.

This needs only to be boiled. . . .

Jesus, let me hear you hush
The ocean lapping on the rocks.
The winds which point the dark-blue firs.
The sea-hawk diving on white froth . . .

It is in death I'll bring them Christ
And show his beauty where they strike.
If I must break apart and feed
The forest green, the birch, the hawk,
The snake, my blood will so descend
To change into the roots we eat,
And flash within the roebuck's eye.
My flesh will fall away with fish
And pebbled stone. My bones will start
The buds we bunch for virgin brides:
Et puis, que mon coeur éclate en flammes!

I will turn upon myself,
And change my ashes sinew-white.

Priez-le, mon cher frère . . .
                              Je suis, etc.

I'll drown the Kennebec with life!

WILLIAM GOODREAU was born in Portland, Maine in 1931. He received his B. A. from Bates College in Lewiston, Maine, and his M. F. A. from the State University of Iowa, where he held an Assistantship for the year 1956-57. He has taught English at the College of Saint Teresa in Winona, Minnesota, since 1957. Mr. Goodreau's poetry has appeared in *The Hudson Review, The Commonweal* and *The Colorado Quarterly*.